Lessons For The Little Girl

Lessons to learn, to live, and to love

ॐ ♥ ॐ

Jaime A. Gill

Lessons For The Little Girl

Lessons to learn, to live, and to love

ঽ ♥ ঽ

Jaime A. Gill

220 Publishing

Chicago, Illinois
220 Publishing
(A Division of 220 Communications)

Published by 220 Publishing
(A Division of 220 Communications)
PO Box 8186
Chicago, IL 60680-8186
www.220communications.com
www.twitter.com/220publishing

Cover design by Bernadette Barksdale-Ivory
www.bbeeivery.wix.com/bbeephotography

Inside layout by Julie M. Holloway
www.jmhcre8ive.com

ISBN 978-1-630-68062-6

Printed in the United States of America

This book is dedicated to:

My Grandmothers Lucille Harris and Lula Gill
My Mother Janice A. Smith
My Sister Lita Gill-Waters
My Aunt Maxine Westmoreland
My Aunt Gail Little
My God-Mother Glenda Golden
My God-Sister Lisa Jones
My Neighbor Ruthie Tyus
Thank you all for nurturing and loving this little girl.

To my beautiful nieces:
Jaqe Gill, Eunique Gill, Hamidah Muhammad-Walker,
Destiny Anderson, Khalidah Muhammad, Salimah Muhammad,
Maryam Muhammad, Aakirah Muhammad, Elicia Best,
Ermoni Best, Krystal Golden, Jasmine Jones, Rayzine Jones…
You are my daily motivation

To My Spiritual Daughters:
Stephanie Johnson, Janae Lacey, Ashley Tolbert…
You are my daily inspiration

To My Media Babies: Akyrah Poston, Diamond Pierce,
Aaliyah Jackson, Kia Jackson, , Ebone Knowles, Whitney Knowles,
Janiece Dyer, Daja Jackson, Tiffani Murphy,
Brittany Nunnery, and Nicole Lynch…
You are my daily reminders

To My Mentee: Tierra Clark…**You are my reflection**

Special Thanks To: Sydney Conway and Jayden Conway for being
my teen review team. Your input helped me to refine my focus and to
remember my dream.

May all of you always listen to and love the little girl inside of you!

Table of Contents (Lesson Locator)

Foreword

Some of the most precious and foundational moments in a woman's life happen as a little girl. It is as little girls that our worlds are shaped and established from a myriad of experiences that ultimately determine who we will be as women.
Although we grow and change, find triumph and defeat and journey through love and loss, the fragments of that "little girl" remain at the center of our lives, impacting the decisions we make, the way we see ourselves, and the lives we choose to live. However, despite what we may have gone through, or what our "little girl" may have felt, within each situation lies a lesson. A lesson to learn. A lesson to live. And a lesson to love.

Lessons for the Little Girl is an introspective look at those lessons, and the power they have to serve as guides for not just our own lives, but for the lives of those we are assigned to touch. What once was a place of confusion is morphed into a place of victory through Jaime's commitment to God and using her life's lessons to inspire others.

The Bible teaches us that our victories lie in our willingness to share our testimony as a means of lending our strength to those who need it as they find themselves in various life predicaments. Our story is not for us, but for those who need the hope and guidance found within it.

- ***Stephanie Brewer***
Author of Wingless Butterfly

Preface

The Search for the Little Girl

The Lessons Begin

Excuse me stranger.....can you help me? I am looking for a little girl.

What does she look like? Well she looks a lot like me actually, but of course, a lot younger. She has these beautiful deep brown eyes that seem to shine even in the darkest midnight. Her smile is wide, bright and very contagious! When you see her smile, you can't help but to smile yourself. She has the energy of a child at play, but a spirit so wise you'd think she has been here before.

When was the last time I saw her? Well, I don't recall. It was like she was here and in a blink of an eye she had vanished. I don't know what I'm going to do without her. You must help me find her. Ever since I lost her, I haven't been able to sleep. I think about her constantly and I think I have cried all the tears out of my eyes. She is my inspiration...my spirit...my joy! We have so many dreams together. So many things we have planned to do. Without her, I don't think our dreams will ever come true.

Do I have a picture of her? Why yes, I sure do...here it is!!

What do you mean you have seen her? Where? When? Is she ok? TAKE ME TO HER!!! What do you mean, the answer is within? I'm the little girl, and the little girl is me? Stranger...what do you mean? OH I SEE!!!

I AM THE LITTLE GIRL, I have just evolved. I thought she had left me, but she has not gone at all! I couldn't see her because I allowed situations, circumstances, and people to distract me. Yet, she has been there all the time. I neglected her to spend time with others and tend to their needs; all the while I was neglecting THE LITTLE GIRL INSIDE OF ME.

Little girl, I'm sorry that I've spent so much time ignoring you. I didn't realize the damage that I was doing; I didn't have a clue. I am you...and you are me! You are the truth that few people get to see. You are my essence, my atom, the core of who I am. God put you here so that I will complete His plans.

Stranger, thank you for showing me my little girl; I couldn't have found her without you. You have allowed me to see that all this time THE LITTLE GIRL WAS INSIDE OF ME!

Often in life we want to know our purpose or we can't figure out what to do, just ask THE LITTLE GIRL THAT IS INSIDE OF YOU! God tells them the answers to all the questions we have. They are what link our future to our past. They are the courage that steps out on faith. They are the ones not afraid to learn from mistakes. They are the ones that love freely and tell the truth. They are our center, our core, our root!

They are the essence to who we REALLY ARE and they help us to become what GOD WANTS US TO BE. So no matter what my age, my little girl will always live inside of me. SHE IS MY TRUE IDENTITY!

Introduction

I wrote *IN SEARCH OF THE LITTLE GIRL* on March 4, 2005. That's right; the date was 03-04-05. I was riding on the train early in the morning on my way to my internship at a Chicago television news station. Although I was a college student and in my twenties, going downtown always allowed me to feel like a little girl going on a field trip. Seeing all the tall buildings and people going to their various destinations always brought me great excitement.

On this particular day, I saw a group of kids on the train who appeared to be a class going on a field trip. They looked at me with the same curiosity I was looking at everyone else. *"Where does she work? What tall building will she be going into?"*

As I looked at one little girl and she looked back at me, I realized that although we were different people, different ages, and even different races, we were both girls, which made me feel connected to her. Then I began to think about all of the young girls that I have interacted with in my community and in my travels. Although I am an adult, I feel like I can still deeply relate to little girls. The feelings, the emotions, the confusion, the dreams; I remember them all so clearly.

This book, *"Lessons for the Little Girl"* is for all girls from middle school to retirement age. The reality is that no matter how old we get, we can still remember when we were little girls. When we are happy we still laugh like that little girl. When we are sad we still cry like that little girl; and ultimately we still want to be loved and dream big like that little girl. These lessons are lessons that you need to learn and embrace throughout your life so that no matter where you are, you can always love and learn a LESSON FOR THE LITTLE GIRL.

Lesson One

The Seed

I grew up in the suburb of Markham, Illinois, a community where we all knew each other and looked out for one another. It was a neighborhood where the older kids played basketball in each other yards or just hung out in the front lawn. While the younger children rode their bikes through the neighborhood and made several trips a day to the candy store. As a little girl I had so much fun going to the park with my friends. I thought I had the best house in the neighborhood because I lived directly in front of the park. I could see the park from both my bedroom and my living room windows. It was like living across the street from Disney World. No matter how many times I went to the park, I always looked forward to the next time I would go.

Whether I was playing on the swings, spinning on the merry-go round until I was dizzy, or catching fireflies when it began to get dark, the park always created hours of fun for me and my friends. One of our favorite things to do was to pick dandelions. I used to call them "cotton ball flowers." My friends and I would pull them from the ground, make a wish, and then blow on them until all of the cotton-like pieces flew away. I used to think that my wishes were flying away to become true and then return to me - another Cabbage Patch doll, a bike, more dresses or games; whatever I had wished for. As I got older, I realized that what I had been calling cotton balls were actually seeds. As I blew on them, or as the wind pulled them from the stem, they were carried away until they drifted to the ground. Over time those seeds would become another dandelion. That meant my wishes were carried away on a seed.

As an adult, that process causes me to think of things that I was taught, such as "treat others the way you want to be treated," or "give and it shall be given unto you." This is truly my dandelion experience.

As a little girl there was so much I dreamt for and wanted for my life. The dandelion taught me that I had to plant the right "seed" to get the results that I desired. If I wanted good grades, my seed was paying attention in class, studying, doing my homework, and passing tests. If I wanted a good job, the seed was to be a strong worker who produced and was able to get along with others.

All flowers come from seeds. Seeds must be planted in dirt in order to grow and blossom into a flower. In our lives there will be times of "dirt" and "rain," times when things aren't so easy. These are the times that nourish and strengthen the "seed," enabling it to sprout and break through the "dirt". Know that the challenges that you face are a necessary part of the process. A flower needs dirt and water; the same is true about your dreams. Once the flower blooms and the dreams come true, it creates an opportunity for another seed to be planted.

Lesson For The Little Girl:

Learn to only plant the "seeds" that you want to grow.

What is it that you want in your life? Recognizing that it will take a

"seed" to be planted first – what seed are you going to plant?

_____

_____

_____

_____

_____

_____

_____

_____

Lesson Two

Nature Speaks

The red cardinal has been my favorite bird since I was a little girl. I love its vibrant color and how it sits on a tree branch and turns its little head from side to side as if it were looking for something.

I wrote a poem about a red cardinal when I was in college. It was my third year, but my first year away from home and my family. For me, this was my first real transition into adulthood – no longer living at home with my mom. I remember sitting on the lawn outside of the dorm thinking about my life: who I was, where I was in my life, and who I wanted to be.

Although my time away from home was going well, I still had days of loneliness, even fear, about my future. I wanted my family to be proud of me and I wanted to be proud of myself. Yet, the pressure that I was applying to myself was beginning to become more overwhelming. Due to the fact that I had class in the morning, I felt as if I could not run away. So, I thought sitting outside to get fresh air was the next best option to me. With my favorite blanket wrapped around my shoulders, I walked to the picnic table nearest to my dorm and sat down.

It was midnight on a weekday, so the campus was very dark and quiet. As I stared at the beautiful campus, how the light of the moon was shining ever so lightly on the side of the chapel, a cardinal flew in front of me. It landed on a statue and it appeared as if it was looking directly at me. I had never seen a bird flying at night before, so the cardinal's presence came as both a surprise and a delight.

This bird reminded me of when I was a little girl looking through my Grandpa Joe's binoculars, pretending to be a professional bird watcher. I would search with great excitement to see how many birds I could find through the trees. Grandpa Joe would always ask me to describe the birds to him and we would jokingly give each bird a name. These were some of my favorite times with my grandfather when I was a little girl. Sitting on my college campus several years later, the presence of the cardinal and the memories of my grandfather brought me great comfort.

As the bird and I sat and stared at each other, I realized that although I was going through a tough time, I had so many happy times to remember and to look forward to. As I smiled, the cardinal suddenly flew away. What a wonderful midnight surprise! Surrounded by the dark night, a little red cardinal brought me so much light.

Lesson For The Little Girl:

Nature surrounds us giving us comfort in the midst of fear,

reminding us that God who seems so far away is always near.

Spend some time paying attention to nature.

What do you see? What can you learn from nature?

_____

_____

_____

_____

_____

_____

_____

Lesson Three

Connect-the-Dots

One of my favorite indoor games as a little girl was connect-the dots. I considered it a simple pleasure. I enjoyed drawing a line from dot to dot to connect them until the last number is reached. After all the dots are connected, a picture is clearly revealed.

In my travels, I've encountered people from many cultures and backgrounds. I would not be who I am today without each encounter. It has given me the opportunity to experience life through music, art, food, education business, religion, and culture in many different ways. It has broadened my perspective and enhanced my life. I wish that people would appreciate the beauty in the differences that exist in this world. The big picture only comes into clear view after there is connection.

In junior high school, we were given class projects and team building activities that were designed for us work together. There were always the people who did their share of the work; while there were others who managed to avoid the work altogether. No matter what, each person's presence in the group mattered. Their presence influenced how we worked and how we communicated. We were forced to work together, because we all wanted a good grade. Whatever our thoughts or opinions, we learned to connect to get the job done.

The same principles apply as I work in different environments as an adult. Each person has a different perspective of what should be done and how it should be done. The beauty is learning how to not only hear each person, but to value each person and their opinions, whether you agree with them or not.

The elements of teamwork and connection are always important. This is the foundation of networking which helps ideas to come to life, business to grow, friendships to develop, and love to blossom. Each connection is a like one dot in connect-the-dots or a puzzle piece; they each hold the information that will connect you to the next. If any dot or piece is missing the picture is incomplete. This is a reminder to each of us that we all are valuable and our differences are beautiful and necessary.

Lesson For The Little Girl:

A beautiful picture is created when we connect to one another.

Who are you connected to?

What picture is created with these connections?

Do you like the picture?

_____

_____

_____

_____

_____

_____

_____

Lesson Four

Problem Solving

Look at the dog lick the bone,

And over there stands a man all alone.

I see the baby wiggling his toes;

Right next to the blooming white rose.

That one looks like a pillow where I can rest my head;

Maybe I can play in that big castle instead.

There are so many things that I see when I am looking into the sky,

As I watch the white puffy clouds pass by.

White clouds in a blue sky;

Looks like cotton balls floating in the sea.

I wonder what the clouds see, when they look down at me.

My backyard was one of my favorite parts of my house when I was a little girl. I loved to lie in my backyard and look up and watch the clouds float slowly over my house. The longer I stared at the clouds, the more they became pictures right before my very eyes. What first looked like nothing, with another glance became something.

I would encounter this lesson again in college with my good friend Kristy, as we were looking for something to eat for dinner. Neither one of us had money to eat out, so we had to figure out another solution. The canned vegetables and the packaged noodles in the back of our closets instantly became like a Thanksgiving feast. It was not our first choice for a meal option so we did not consider it initially. After quickly realizing we had no other options for food, we both reconsidered. What we originally thought was nothing became something major for two very hungry college students.

Having the ability to make the minimal work is a lesson throughout life that can always be applied. Whether you have to get something done in a short amount of time, or you are trying to take care of bills with minimal funds; limited resources should not mean limited effort or creativity to solve a problem. A positive outlook is necessary to all types of problem solving; for it is not about what you see, but rather how you see it. Do not allow laziness, negativity, or the reality of the solution not being easy for you, cause you to give up. It is in these situations that you think harder and work harder to solve the problem, no matter what it is. Ask yourself how much do you want it? How much does it mean to you? You will discover anything worth having is worth working for.

No matter what the situation you are facing know that everything is not as it may first appear. You may need to go back and take a second look; for what you were looking for may have been right in front of you all the time.

Lesson For The Little Girl:

What you see as nothing is really something waiting to be seen from a different perspective.

What situation in your life do you need to look at differently?

_____

_____

_____

_____

_____

_____

_____

_____

_____

_____

Lesson Five

Legacy

I loved spending time with my grandparents. Not only because they would usually give me whatever I wanted, but I loved hearing stories about their lives and the challenges and successes they experienced while growing up. Although it was hard for me to always realize, my grandparents were not always grandparents. They were once little boys and little girls who were young like me and had dreams, goals, and even some fears.

As I look at pictures of my grandparents in their younger years, I can't help but wonder if we were alike as children. What was their favorite subject in school? What types of friends did they have? What were their career aspirations? How did Grandpa know that Grandma was the girl he wanted to marry and start a family with?

It is fun to remember how my Grandfather James, who we all called "Grandpa Joe," and I loved to eat chicken and rice and watch old movies. My Grandma Lucille, who I loved to call "My Lucy," loved to take me shopping and dance to music.

Grandpa Mack would always give me a $2 dollar bill as he sat in his favorite chair; while Grandma Lula would share her favorite recipes and stories about all the statues she collected. Grandpa O.P. gave all the grandkids a nick-name. I thought mine was the best: "Little Mama."

All of my grandparents have passed away, but I have so many memories of each of them that make me stronger. I know it was one of their greatest desires to always provide for me and to create opportunities for me to be whatever I dreamed to be. They always believed I could achieve great success.

I carry each of my grandparents in my heart every day: remembering their stories, the sounds of their laughs, and the warmth of their hugs. I know that as I continue to learn and grow, their spirit continues to live. Their legacy is me!

I realize that not everyone has a healthy and happy relationship with their grandparents or other family members, but that does not mean there is nothing to learn from them. Learning how to create better relationships with your family members is very important. No situation is impossible. Realize that everyone behaves based off their experiences. Take into consideration the possible experiences in their lives that may have led them to respond the way that they do; just as your experiences guide your thoughts and behaviors. For the individuals that you are having difficulty with or for those family members that have passed away, you can utilize the opportunity to create stronger relationships with others in the family.

Lesson For The Little Girl:

You are the legacy to HER and HIS STORY.

Write something your grandparents' lives have taught you.

_____

_____

_____

_____

_____

_____

_____

_____

_____

_____

_____

Lesson Six

Capture

During the holidays I love looking at family pictures and home videos. We enjoy laughing at each other's clothes and hairstyles, but most importantly we enjoy reliving moments that were captured on film.

In one of my favorite home movies, I am seven years old and celebrating with my Grandma Lucy, Mom, and sister Lita, while Grandpa O.P. was filming with his new camera. Watching the video always brings me so much joy.

One of my favorite scenes is when my sister and I tried to teach Grandma Lucy some dance moves. I laugh every time, as if I was watching the video for the first time. I am so glad that I have this video to look at and remember my Grandmother's beautiful face or to hear my Grandfather's funny laugh. It is funny to see how I always followed my sister around and how I loved to watch my Mom dance. Although that time has passed, I can relive it every time I watch the video.

With the constant growth in technology, it is so easy to capture family time with our smartphones and digital cameras. Along with the creation of social networking and user friendly editing programs, we are able to create and chronicle special moments in our lives in the most creative ways. Why is this so important? Well, let's think about it. Throughout history we are able to see scenes of years and events that have passed because of our ability to capture it.

Telling the story through newspapers and journals are enhanced by the visual image of photography and film. To be able to see the faces of the people behind the story allows you to realize the significance of their presence. From celebratory events such as the history of movie making or the election of former leaders, to the more tragic parts of history such as wars, visual media is not only a part of world history, but your personal history.

Remembering a loved one's smile is one thing, but to be able to re-experience it through a photo or a video clip means so much more. Taking a moment to capture the moments can really last a lifetime and beyond.

Lesson For The Little Girl:

Take a moment to capture the moments that will last only for a while but can be treasured forever.

Place a picture of one of your favorite moments here and write the

importance of this moment to you.

_____

_____

_____

_____

_____

_____

_____

_____

Lesson Seven

Against All Odds

When I was four years old my mother came home with a bulletin from the park district, asking me what sport I wanted to learn to play that summer. I come from a very athletic family. My uncle, James A. Smith Jr., played professional football in the NFL. Both of my brothers, Tony and Patrick, played basketball and football; and my sister Lita was a cheerleader, played basketball, softball and participated in track and field. My parents and grandparents were also very athletic, golfing and bowling even after retirement. So, it was only fitting that I played sports as well.

Although softball and basketball were the most popular sports among the girls in the neighborhood, I wanted to try the new tennis program. I had no idea that what I considered to be a random choice would become a vital part of my life for more than 25 years.

As a sophomore in high school, I was on the varsity tennis team. During the final tournament of the year, I was competing in the last match of the day, playing against the toughest team in the tournament. My winning, or losing, would determine if my team would win the conference championship. I had to admit that this added additional pressure to my mind about winning.

With my coach and teammates' words of encouragement echoing behind me on the other side of the fence, I remember walking to the base line of the tennis court, closing my eyes, and remembering my first tennis coach, Mr. Brunson.

Mr. Brunson was concerned about whether or not I was going to be able to play tennis because I was so knock-kneed and my toes pointed toward one another. He was afraid I would fall over my feet. Yet, he saw my willingness to learn, my passion for the game, with a huge desire to win. He said that I always seemed like I was having fun, which I was. Mr. Brunson instilled in me not to let winning become more important than doing my best and having fun. As a coach, he was committed to training and teaching me everything he knew to make me a strong tennis player and a strong person.

Eleven years later, I was at the top of my game with an opportunity to bring the trophy home; not just for me, but for my entire team and my high school. It was a great match! Although it was challenging, I enjoyed every moment of it. I was ecstatic when I won the match and we were given the championship trophy.

As I held the trophy, tears of joy streamed down my face because I couldn't help but think that if I had allowed the direction my feet pointed to stop me at age 4, I would not have been able to hold the conference tennis championship trophy at 15. Mr. Brunson taught a very valuable lesson to this little girl; a lesson that has carried me through my toughest challenges on and off the court. No matter what the odds may be against you, perspective and attitude in every situation is important in order to be victorious.

Lesson For The Little Girl:

Never give up on your dreams no matter what obstacles you face.
The things that may be the most difficult will be your training to win
your race.

What challenges may be preparing you to accomplish your dream?

_____

_____

_____

_____

_____

_____

_____

_____

_____

_____

_____

Lesson Eight

Creating Your Own Space

Living in a 3 bedroom house with my mom, my sister and two brothers, meant that I had to share a room with my sister who is 8 years older than I am, for many years of my childhood. I had to be very creative in trying to claim my space. Despite the age difference, my sister and I did have a lot of things in common, so we were able to agree with some decorating ideas. On the other hand, there were definitely some differences, so I had to be creative in creating my own space in our shared space.

It wasn't until my mom and I moved to Richton Park, Illinois during my sophomore year of high school when I received my very own room. Finally, I had my own space to decorate the way that I wanted to. No longer did I have to share closet space, drawer space, or desk space with someone else.

Throughout my childhood, I dreamed about having my own space. When we moved in I had no idea how I was going to decorate because I never had so much space to myself before. I finally decided that I wanted my room to reflect my personality, celebrate my hobbies, and promote my dreams. With this in mind, I decorated my room with lots of pictures of family and friends, next to my collage of pictures of the dynamic tennis sister duo, Venus and Serena Williams, along with my collection of Betty Boop figurines. My comforter and curtains were the perfect accent with its bold and bright colors.

As an adult, I still love to decorate with pictures and bright colors in my office space and at home. These elements inspire and comfort me. It is important that, no matter how large your home, bedroom, or office space is, make sure that the environment is conducive to what you want to do in that space. You want your bedroom to be relaxing, comforting, and clean to help you rest well at night. You want your work space to be neat and organized, so that you can find what you need when you need it. You will see an organized and creative space helps to inspire creativity and generates positive energy.

Lesson For The Little Girl:

Every space has energy – create a space that will inspire you.

How do you feel in your space?

What can you add or remove to help your space inspire you more?

Chapter Nine

Adventures of Reading

I love to read! I always have. When I have free time, I sit in my room for hours and read chapter after chapter until I finish the book cover to cover. When I was a little girl I kept a collection of books in the back seat of my mother's car, just in case we would be gone from the house for several hours. From *Curious George* to *The Adventures of the Baby Sitter's Club,* I absolutely loved connecting to the characters and feeling as if I actually knew them and lived in the same town with them.

With every book I read I wanted to read more. I went from reading small animated books to longer novels. I felt as if I could travel all over the world from my bedroom with the turn of a page. Reading was not just fun, it was also an escape from my world. No matter what kind of day I was having, reading always made it better. My imagination allowed me to see pictures that the words described allowing me to see scenes in vivid detail.

Reading is still one of my favorite forms of entertainment and escape. It also serves as an opportunity to learn and to understand ideas, concepts, other cultures, and things about the world. From the pages of a book or from the screen of an e-reader, I can become a student of life, gaining information at my fingertips.

It fascinates me how letters become words and words become sentences that help the world communicate and learn. Books serve as an opportunity for education as well as entertainment that enhances our ability to know more about ourselves and the very diverse world that we live in.

When I was a little girl, there was a television show I watched faithfully, *The Reading Rainbow*. One of the lyrics to the theme song was:

> *Take a look; it's in a book – The Reading Rainbow.*

I loved this show and the theme song, because it brought the stories that I read in black and white ink to my television in color. Reading helped stretch my imagination as I imagined the characters' faces, their clothes, and their behaviors. Reading at a young age also taught me the importance of sharing information with others.

Throughout history there were *griots*, or those who told stories from generation to generation about the history of a culture. The stories of our history went from being verbally communicated to written, so that information would not be lost and could reach more people.

As little girls grow into young adults and then adults, reading often goes from being a hobby to work; reading text books for a test or new manuals at work. Although the basic element of reading is required every day as we read directions, recipes and text messages, none of these compare to the experience of allowing a book to relax the mind, enhance our vocabulary, and teach us the power of human language.

Reading is a tool that allows a message to be carried from one source to the next. From the heart and mind of the author to the reader, information can be carried across time and distance. For reading is more than pages of words, it is a window of opportunity for discovery.

Lesson For The Little Girl:

The more you read, the more you know.

The more you know, the more you grow.

What is your favorite book? What did it teach you?

_____

_____

_____

_____

_____

_____

_____

_____

_____

Chapter Ten

Self-Care

Bath time as a little girl always meant play time for me. I loved taking baths. I would gather up my doll collection and put their swimsuits on so that my bath time could be their swimming time. I'd sit in the tub playing so long that my fingertips and toes would become wrinkled like raisins.

Bath time was also an opportunity for relaxation. My mother and Grandma Lucy made sure that they filled my bath water with the best soaps and skin care products that cleaned and nourished my skin.

As I got older, I never forgot the relaxation of bath time. Although I no longer brought my toys to the tub, I recognized the importance of healthy self-care. If a car needs regular car maintenance and wax treatments, then surely the human body requires regular maintenance and care.

Consistent skin care with the right products for your skin will help limit acne, blemishes, and dry skin. We must take care of the skin that we are in, and the sooner we start, the better. The ability to create HEALTHY self-care, from the inside out, can increase your strength, energy, and enhance your sense of self value. Often women compare themselves to others in order to define beauty. This is the worst method of measurement. Your individual beauty can never be compared to that of another individual; for we are each beautiful in different ways. A beautiful inside must be matched with a beautiful and healthy inside. Healthy is about functionality – being free from illness or injury.

Consistent self-care also consists of eating necessary portions of fruits and vegetables, drinking plenty of water, along with plenty of exercise and rest. These elements will help you live a healthier and stronger life. Allowing time to sleep, turning your cell phone off, television off, and allowing your body to "disconnect" and rest, helps energize both body and mind.

Mental, emotional, and spiritual care are equally as important as physical care. You can have a physically healthy and strong body, but not have a healthy mind or spirit. Thinking more positively, surrounding yourself with people and situations that build you up versus tearing you down, journaling, and praying, are just a few examples of how to strengthen your mind, your spirit and balance your emotions.

Created as nurturers, females have the desire to take care of and be concerned about everyone around us, unfortunately while neglecting ourselves. The better you take care of yourself, the greater the capacity to be able to give to someone else. Also, by taking care of yourself you are able to show others how valuable you **KNOW** you are. People will only treat you the way that you allow them to; and often it is based on how they see YOU treat or take care of YOURSELF.

With the many dreams and aspirations that you have, you have to be healthy and strong enough to endure the tasks required to accomplish your goals. Taking care of yourself allows for total health, because being healthy inside and out is indeed a beautiful thing.

Lesson For The Little Girl:

Choose Better. Do Better. Live Better. Feel Better.

What are some habits that you can include in your schedule to

increase your self- care?

_____

_____

_____

_____

_____

_____

_____

_____

_____

_____

Lesson Eleven

Start Now

I remember it like it was yesterday. I was sitting in the car with my Godmother Glenda. She was helping me prepare for my first public speech. I was going to be speaking at her church at a luncheon. I remember sitting there with my pretty dress on and my little black Bible in my hand. As I practiced my lines over and over, I remembered my Godmother telling me, "Speak from your heart". These words have served as a reminder to me throughout my life. As I speak across the country to teens and women's groups, or even as a radio talk show host, I always remember to "speak from my heart."

I am sure my Godmother Glenda did not realize that the words and coaching she gave to me as a six year old, would still be with me almost 30 years later, and be the beginning of a lifetime career and a passion for public speaking. I learned at six years old that I loved public speaking. I loved being able to connect with people, by sharing a message of hope and inspiration.

Despite your age, you are the right age to start pursuing your dreams. Age, finances, people, or situations should never be an excuse to keep you from pursuing your dreams. Every day that you wake up is another day to work towards your dreams. There are instances when someone very young passes away. On the other hand someone else may live to be over the age of 100. This shows you that you don't know when you last moment alive will be. Therefore, every day that you wake up is the perfect day to pursue your dreams. Realize that your dreams and aspirations are not just about you. There are people connected to your dreams. While you delay because you think you are not the right age, someone is waiting for you to make the dream a reality.

Whether your dream is to write a book, create a cure for cancer, to be a teacher, singer, wife, parent, politician, dancer, fitness trainer, or even just a kind and compassionate person...someone will benefit from your dreams. If it is one person or thousands, to know that **YOU CAN MAKE A DIFFERENCE** is worth you starting. Better to start and know, than not to begin and wonder. Your dreams are waiting for you to make them come true. There is no time better than NOW, for it is all you have.

Lesson For The Little Girl:

Now is the best time!

What is your dream? Make a plan of what you can begin to do

today to make your dreams come true?

_____

_____

_____

_____

_____

_____

_____

_____

_____

_____

Lesson Twelve

Surprise! Surprise!

I love surprises! I always have and I always will. Being surprised with a present or being taken somewhere I always wanted to go always makes me feel good. Since I loved surprises, my Jack-in-the-box toy always gave me great enjoyment as a little girl. A clown is closed inside of a box. When the handle on the side of the colorful box is turned, music begins to play and eventually the clown comes bouncing out of the box on a spring. The clown would surprise me every time. I would try to count how many times I needed to turn the handle before the clown would bounce out, but it changed every time.

The jack-in-the-box is a lot like life – FULL OF SURPRISES! Unfortunately, all of the surprises won't make you laugh or feel good. Sometimes people get sick – surprise! Car accidents happen, people disappoint us, plans get canceled, loved ones pass away, it rains on the day of your party- SURPRISE! Know that both the good and the bad surprises may not always be expected, but it causes us to think "outside of the box." It teaches us how to be resourceful and exercise our faith and strength.

If the surprise is finding out you were hired at a new job or finding out that you were getting fired, each situation is an opportunity to grow! Life is full of surprises, but like the jack-in-the-box, you have to keep turning and you have to be willing to spring at any situation and handle it with a smile. This is not always easy, but it is very necessary. Think about a situation in your past that you thought was impossible, or that you would never get passed. You have passed that time and you survived that situation. I am sure that you not only learned some things for that seemingly impossible situation, but you are now stronger because of it. SURPRISE!!!

Lesson For The Little Girl:

Surprises are a major ingredient to the formula of life.

What is the most memorable surprise you have experienced?

_____

_____

_____

_____

_____

_____

_____

_____

_____

_____

_____

Lesson Thirteen

Money Management

I loved that my Grandpa Joe's house was not far from my house in Markham. When my mom felt I was old enough, she allowed me to ride my bike or scooter to his house. The great thing about the route to his house was that I would pass two candy stores. I would always stop at both of them because one candy store always had something that the other one didn't. One of the best things about the candy stores when I was a little girl was that you could purchase candy for a penny, five cents or ten cents. A person could get a lot of candy for one dollar!

Very early I began to realize the importance of managing my money. I could have easily spent all of my allowance at the candy store. However, that meant that I would not have any money for anything else that I may have wanted to buy later. Money management is an important habit to have and it is a habit that can always be enhanced. As you get older, decisions may not be how much candy to buy at the candy store, but rather buying a home, a car, designer shoes, or purse The earlier you learn how to manage a little, the easier it will be to manage more.

As I look at my own journey with money management, there have been times when I was irresponsible with my money by focusing more on my wants, instead of my needs or savings. I usually felt very defeated and discouraged afterwards. I knew that my financial situation would never change if I never changed my mind or my habits. I had to make more responsible decisions, such as writing down all of my purchases, and saving my receipts. I also learned that I had to take care of my responsibilities before I indulged in purchases that I wanted. I could not be afraid to save. In fact, saving is necessary!

With growth also comes insight, and I realized the importance of my credit score. A credit score for an adult is like a grade point average for a student (GPA). It is an indicator of your ability at managing your financial responsibilities. Much like a GPA, your credit score allows you access to other opportunities; such as receiving better deals to buying a home, car, obtaining a loan, or even receiving a job.

Along with changing my mind and my habits, I also had to change my money language. Making statements like: "I'm broke," or "I don't have any money," had to stop being responses to my money situation. Instead, using statements like: "That is not in my budget right now;" or "I'm saving for something else;" allow you to feel more empowered about your money situation.

Changing your daily actions with money will also help in changing your money management. Do you put your money in your wallet or purse neatly? Do you balance your check book? Do you know how much money is in your bank account(s)? Do you write down your purchases? Do you save your receipts? Do you have a savings account? Doing all of the above allows you to be better money managers. Know where your money is and where it is going. Manage your money; don't allow it to manage you.

.

Lesson For The Little Girl:

Learning to save is just as important as learning to make a smart buy.

How do you feel about your current spending/saving habits? How can you strengthen your thinking and habits in money management?

_____

_____

_____

_____

_____

_____

_____

_____

_____

_____

Lesson Fourteen

Friendships

I've always been blessed to have friends from all over the world. From childhood to adulthood, I've always enjoyed the opportunity to meet new people, learn about them, their lives, their families-even their cultures. I always believed that there is so much to learn from those who are raised differently from you. In fact, there is joy in learning and appreciating the differences as much as the similarities.

When I was in high school, I loved the diversity of friendships that I had. One group of friends that I enjoyed spending time with included Sam, whose family is from India, Adelle, whose family is from Ghana, and Kim, whose family is from Poland, France and Norway. We would take turns spending the night at one another's homes, learning about each other's family traditions and culture.

We had so much fun being with one another and learning about each other. Here's the funny thing: the more we learned about each other, the more we learned about ourselves. Whether we were eating hotdog hash, curried chicken or homemade desserts, my friendships with these girls helped me to appreciate my friends completely.

My best friend Joy and I have known each other since we were three and four years of age. Even as we grew up over the years and college separated us, the different experiences we had separately allowed us to treasure the times we had together as well as introduce new things to one another. Now as Joy works as a pediatrician and I work in television, even our career differences add character to our friendship. I have learned from Joy, Sam, Adelle, Kim and many other friends from childhood that true friendship is not about having everything in common, but also being willing to embrace things that are different.

Someone's differences take nothing away from you; actually it adds to you. It gives you insight, exposure, and opportunities to realize how big and diverse the world is, and how much there is to learn and experience.

Imagine if all of your clothes in your closet looked exactly the same: same color, same fabric, and same style. At some point you would get tired of looking the same way absolutely every day. Some clothing makes you feel happy, sporty, or even professional. The diversity of clothing enhances your personality. Such is true of the diversity in your friendships. Don't be stuck on having friends that all look like you and think like you. You always need a friend that will challenge you and strengthen you. There is an old saying that states, "If you are the smartest person in you group, you need to get a new group."

Your friends should be able to teach you some things, and have some strengths and abilities that you don't have.

As I look at all my beautiful friends, those of the past and those current, each of them make me a stronger and better person because I learned to value our differences, as much as our similarities.

Lesson For The Little Girl:

Friendships are some of life's greatest treasures. The diversity in those friendships can teach us new things and show us the joy in diversity.

What are some things you have in common with your closest

friends? What are some of your differences?

What have you learned from them?

_____

_____

_____

_____

_____

_____

_____

_____

Lesson Fifteen

Decision Making

Every day our lives are filled with decisions we must make: what to wear, what to eat, what to watch on TV. With every decision there is a result or a consequence. It is important to create a habit of healthy decision making by considering the possible positive or possible negative outcomes. Maybe there will not be a negative outcome, maybe just one not as favorable for you. For example, you can choose to go to Florida or California for vacation. Both are great options for you to have fun and enjoy great weather, but one trip may cost more than the other, depending on your mode of travel and your plans once you arrive.

Knowledge is information. Wisdom is the proper application of information. When making decisions, you cannot allow your emotions to be your only guide. If we are angry, we may react to a particular situation one way; but when we are happy, we respond to the same scenario differently. The problem is that our feelings are always changing.

Sometimes because of the weather, how people in our lives treat us, how much money we have or don't have, or because of something that someone said to us; our emotions can change in an instant. To make decisions based only on our feelings can cause more problems in the long run.

I remember playing in my backyard as a little girl, and my older sister Lita was my babysitter. She told me that my playtime was over and that I had to come in the house and get ready for dinner. I was not ready to stop playing so I made the decision to ignore her. After Lita demanded I come in for the second time, I went into the house, bringing a very bad attitude along with me. My sister continued telling me how important it was that I obeyed her as the one my mom left in charge. I did not like what she had to say, so I made the decision to take a hand-held chalkboard and threw it at her.

It happened so fast! It hit her face, but thankfully it did not cause any permanent damage. I was so angry about her ending my play time that I made a decision, based on my emotions, to throw something at her. If my sister had been hurt, it would have devastated me. I love my sister more than I loved playing outside, but my decision did not reflect that. I had to learn that things may not always go the way I want or the way I think they should, but I must make responsible and healthy decisions.
A situation can change simply because of the way you decide to respond. The power is truly in your decision making.

You can control your decisions but we can't control the consequences to your decisions. Learn to choose better so you can do better in order to *be* better, and then you **will** live better. Even what you consider a "small decision" will be great practice for your "bigger decisions." Small decisions may be considered: taking care of your work before enjoying time with your friends; choosing to eat a piece of fruit for a snack instead of always choosing potato chips; choosing to listen more or doing something nice for someone else. Bigger decisions may be: choosing how to respond in an argument, choosing a college to attend, making a career move, deciding who date, choosing where to live, or even deciding the health care of a sick loved one. Making decisions is an activity that we will do every day, several times a day, for the rest of our lives.

In your decision making, always consider the long term effects; not just for you but for others. Due to the fact that you do not live on a planet all by yourself, every decision that you make affects other people, whether you recognize it or not. Let the impact that you have be one that you will be proud of, and that you would want to happen to you.

Lesson For The Little Girl:

Deciding to make healthy decisions is the best decision that you can make.

What is a situation that you know you made the wrong decision? How do you think the situation would have changed if you responded differently?

_____

_____

_____

_____

_____

_____

_____

_____

Lesson Sixteen

Boy Friendships

Since I loved following my sister Lita around when I was a little girl, there were many lessons that I learned from her. She has always been and always will be one of my heroes; and this lesson is one of my favorites.

I followed Lita everywhere! I followed her to her basketball games, when she went to her friend's house, and I even followed her on her dates. She didn't appreciate that too much because her dates ended up spending more time spoiling me than they did interacting with her. Although I received lots of attention and candy on my sister's dates, there was a much more valuable gift I received.

My sister was such a great athlete "for a girl", as the boys would say, that they loved being around her to compete with her on the track field or on the basketball court. The fact that she was also very pretty and smart gave them even more reason to want to be around her. I always thought that my sister would be one of the first women to play in the NBA, or at least to marry an NBA basketball player.

Lita taught me that just because she had things in common with a boy did not mean that she had to date him. As a little girl, I thought it only made sense, if two people were attracted to one another and had things in common, they should date, get married, and live happily ever after. This may be a perfect recipe for a movie script or a fairy tale, but not for real life.

My sister taught me at a very early age that by having male friends, you have the opportunity to learn how they think and behave; so when the time comes and you do begin to date, you know how to interact with them because of the lessons you've learned from your boy FRIENDS.
The reality is you are going to have male classmates, co-workers, neighbors, and bosses, and you don't have to flirt with them, date them, or marry them, because there is attraction or similarities.

Having the ability to choose not to date is just as important as choosing who to date and when. Dating is a responsibility and is more than finding one another attractive. There are many things that are needed foundationally in order to make a dating relationship successful, and those things are developed in having friendships. Is he honest? How does he talk about and treat other ladies? What is his relationship with his mother? Does he respect you? Does he value your dreams and your skills? Can he handle your good days and your bad days? How does he handle conflict? Is his money management healthy? Can he teach you something? Is he positive and encouraging? Is he a good listener?

These are just a few attributes you need to be able to identify and establish in friendship successfully, before preparing to date someone.

It breaks my heart to see girls of all ages feeling like their lives are not complete unless they are in a relationship with a man. Just as devastating is seeing a girl in a relationship where they are not honored and treated as the beautiful, valuable individual that they are. Spending time to get to know a male as a FRIEND also gives you an opportunity to truly know yourself. Often times girls begin dating too young or rush into a relationship too soon, causing more damage to themselves in the long run because they refused to be patient. Focus on growing as an individual before you focus on growing as a unit. Don't rush the process or you will disrupt the progress.

There is so much life to experience and so much to still learn about yourself. As girls, we are beautiful ever evolving people. Embrace the journey and truly learn what it is that you need, like, dislike, can't tolerate, will be willing to compromise on, and can't live without - before rushing into a relationship. When you do meet that special man you will know how to develop a relationship with the tools of: faith, communication, trust, honesty, love, perseverance, and commitment as the foundation, which was developed in your friendship first.

Lesson For The Little Girl:

All of your boy friends don't have to be your **boyfriends**.

In order to get what you want in life, you have to know what you want

and, more importantly, you have to be willing to work towards it

and wait for it, settling for nothing else.

List qualities that are important to you in male friendships.

_____

_____

_____

_____

_____

_____

_____

_____

Lesson Seventeen

The Gift of Forgiveness

"I'm sorry" is one of the most difficult things to say. Apologizing means you have realized that you were wrong about something or have hurt or disappointed someone. Just as difficult to say is, "I forgive you".

You may ask yourself, "Does she really mean it? Will he ever do it again?" There may be hesitations on your part to actually forgive the wrong-doer because you don't want to be hurt or disappointed again. There is a risk in forgiving and being forgiven. Yet, these are two risks that we must take in life. Take the risk of asking for forgiveness and take the risk of forgiving, whether the wrong-doer asks for it or not.

One of the toughest lessons in forgiveness I learned was when a man who assaulted me asked me years later to forgive him. My first thought was to say no, but then I realized that by not forgiving him, I was doing more harm to myself. I was angry, bitter, afraid, and unhappy. I wanted to experience freedom and joy again, so I took the risk and I forgave him, and I meant it. At that moment, I felt like a weight had been removed from my shoulders. He cried and I cried. But more importantly I was able to move forward. No longer was I held captive to the memory of the attack, but I was able to move forward in my life by giving the gift of forgiveness.

Some people think that apologizing or forgiving shows weakness. Actually, it's just the opposite. It shows you have strength to not allow something that happened to continue to affect you, by letting it go and moving forward with a clear heart and mind, in order to bring healing to a situation or relationship. It only adds a greater level of love and compassion to your life. Also, you may need someone to forgive you one day.

Be willing to forgive to the degree that you want to be forgiven. It is not about "forgive and forget;" it is about you forgiving, to release yourself from the weight and anger that not forgiving brings. Forgive them and forgive you! The only thing that a lack of forgiveness brings is a constant reminder of why you chose not to forgive initially. You are reliving the incident over and over. When you forgive, you give yourself the opportunity to heal and move on.

Lesson For The Little Girl:

Forgiveness is a process. Give yourself permission to forgive, which
opens the opportunities for you to be forgiven.

Who do you need to forgive in your life?

_____

_____

_____

_____

_____

_____

_____

_____

_____

_____

Lesson Eighteen

BEautiful You

After telling my friends a joke that really wasn't funny, I began to laugh as if was the best joke. The others began to laugh as well, after seeing me laugh hysterically; not because they thought the joke was funny, but because I thought it was so funny.

One of my friends responded, "You are so silly." I replied, "And proud of it!"

Although it was a very small and brief funny moment with friends, it made me think about my youth and teenage years. Those years were times when I found myself wondering why certain people didn't like me. It was strange that no matter how many friends I had, I focused on the people that didn't like me.

Was it because I wore glasses? Was it because I was taller than the rest of the girls in my class *and* most of the boys? Was it because I lived in a certain area? Did they think I was too big or unattractive?

I remember the times I would hide certain information about myself, just so people would like me. After years of hiding or changing myself, I realized I was not being *MYSELF!*

Unfortunately, it wasn't until I was almost 30 years of age that I began to really love and value myself completely. I love my big nose. I love my long legs. I love my long toes. I love my dimple in my chin. I love my silly sense of humor. I love the glasses I wear. I love my race. I love the fact that I love country music. I love the fact that I like eating Cheetos with my honey buns. I love the fact that I like dipping French fries in my ice cream. I love the fact that I love dancing, even if I am the only one on the dance floor. I love the fact that I am me!

If I waited around for everyone to like me, I would be waiting forever. The reality is that there are some people that are not going to like you no matter what you do or what you look like. You don't have to convince people that you are beautiful, intelligent or valuable. The important thing is that YOU KNOW IT!

Even with the things that I want to strengthen or enhance about myself, I don't beat myself up about them. I choose to actively work on those areas to get better, but not with the goal to convince others to like me. It is to make me a better person for *me*!

Lesson For The Little Girl:

Value yourself – Be true to YOU!

You are the best you there is… You are an original masterpiece!

List some things that you presently love about yourself. Then list

some things that you are going to learn to love about yourself.

_____

_____

_____

_____

_____

_____

_____

_____

_____

Lesson Nineteen

Give Back While Moving Forward

Walking down the hallway of Rich Central, my former high school, brought back so many memories. As I peered into the classrooms, I began to think about some of my favorite teachers and the friendships that began in those classrooms. As I walked past lockers upstairs, I smiled as I thought about my high school crush who didn't even know I existed, because I was a freshman and he was a senior.

I experienced so much in those four years of high school. Then I returned 14 years later to speak to the current students for career day. As I shared information with the students about my career in television production, I also shared stories of my years of being a student at Rich Central, and some of my most memorable experiences. I shared stories of my favorite teachers, some of my most difficult classes, and the fun we had at pep rallies, dances, sporting events, and after school activities.

As the students and I laughed and compared stories of being a Rich Central student, I realized the importance of giving back to the community and environment that helped me to become the woman that I am today. From tutoring, mentoring, picking up garbage on the streets, feeding the homeless, to even helping at a local community center, it is important to give back to show appreciation to those who have helped you. This will serve as a reminder of how far you have come, as well as be motivation to you for where you are going.

Giving back also keeps you grounded and helps you to stay humble. You never want to take your success and achievement for granted. You will also, in turn, become an inspiration to others to never give up on their dreams. Choosing to give back helps you move that much farther forward.

Lesson For The Little Girl:

As you move forward don't forget to give back.

What are some ways you can give back in your community?

_____

_____

_____

_____

_____

_____

_____

_____

_____

_____

_____

_____

_____

Lesson Twenty

Masterpiece

I am created by the Creator to create. Staring at the stars in the sky, trying to see which ones are bigger; wondering how the planets are suspended in space without dropping into darkness, or watching waves crash from the ocean into the shore; there is much in this world to be admired. Viewing the tops of mountains from an airplane, or scuba diving in the ocean with colorful fish swimming all around you; watching a newborn baby sleep, or hearing the laughter of children at play – all are miracles of creation.

No matter how intelligent we are as humans, there is one much greater than our minds - God! Out of all the lessons I learned as a little girl, the most important one was the reality of God and how He created me, you, and all of the things around us.

The difference between the stars, the planets, the waves, the mountains, and the fish, is that God created you (and me) in His image. In each of us, He has placed desires and talents so that we can create here in this world; create books, paintings, buildings, medicines, inventions, cars, and opportunities of hope and love. We are creatures created by the Creator to create. What does that mean?

God has given you a dream and a set of skills for you to give back to the world as a reflection of Him. Out of all the lessons in this book, this lesson is evident throughout all the lessons. Each of the experiences God brings us through is a creative opportunity to express the love of God.

The greatest gift in any situation is to love, because God is love. Therefore, when you display love in a situation, you are acknowledging God's reality. Love your family and your friends. Love your jobs, your community, your neighbors, and even those that hurt you. Learning to love through the hurt and the pain allows God to heal the hurt and the pain. The deepest desire at the core of every little girl is to be loved, and that love is received when we learn how to give love with every lesson and experience.

The mirrors that you see on the top of each lesson page is a constant reminder that we have an opportunity to see God at work in ourselves as we reflect Him and His love in the world-through our actions, our words, and our personalities. The hand that is holding the mirror is symbolic of God's hand, your hand, and my hand; holding up the mirror for you to see all the beauty that you are created to be.

Lesson For The Little Girl:

LOVE IS THE GREATEST LESSON OF ALL!

How can you share more love?

What gift will you give back to the world?

_____

_____

_____

_____

_____

_____

_____

_____

_____

STAY CONNECTED...

I hope that you enjoyed reading **Lessons for the Little Girl.** This is a true outpouring of my heart because of my desire to help every "little girl," no matter what age, to be able to reflect, recognize, and then operate, from their greatest value in which they were created. I want to encourage you to read the book again in six months or a year, to see how you have changed and grown. Life is a journey. Don't get so focused on the destination that you miss the beauty in the journey. One of the most beautiful parts of the journey is self-reflection and self- discovery.

I would love to keep in contact you and hear your feedback about your journey through this book. Please feel free to contact me through my website: **www.jaimeagill.com** . Through my website you will find all of my social networking pages on Facebook, Instagram, and Twitter. If you would like me to come and speak at your next book club meeting, event, or organizational meeting, please send your inquiries through my web page as well. I look forward to hearing from all of you.

Hugs and Love Always,

Jaime A. Gill

Lessons For The Little Girl

Lessons to learn, to live, and to love

୬ ♥ ୬

"A reflective opportunity for every girl to embrace her true identity"

CPSIA information can be obtained at www.ICGtesting.com
Printed in the USA
LVOW01s0235090514

385077LV00011B/117/P